Playtime Activities

Ray Gibson

Designed by Amanda Barlow
Edited by Jenny Tyler
Illustrated by Amanda Barlow
and Michaela Kennard

Photography by Howard Allman and Ray Moller

Contents

I can cut and stick

A truck

1. Cut some squares as big as this book.

2. Fold one in half and in half again. Cut along the folds.

Stick on a window

3. Stick down two big squares and one small one.

Decorate with
strips of paper.
Stick on letters
from magazines.

4. Cut some wheels
from dark paper.

5. Stick them on.
Add foil hub caps.

A caterpillar

1. Open out the flap of an envelope.

2. Fold in half. Cut a "V" to fit your finger.

3. Cut off the corners.

4. Open out. Sponge paint on both sides.

4

5. Cut eyes and a big smile from paper. Stick them on.

Stick fingers through holes.

Flowers and bees

1. Draw a flower with a wax crayon.

2. Cut it out. Stick on a paper middle.

3. Make some more flowers and leaves.

4. Draw bees. Crayon eyes and stripes. Cut bees out.

Stick the wings on the bees.

5. Draw wings. Cut them out.

6. Stick everything down in a pattern.

7

A snake card

1. Fold a long piece of cardboard in half.

2. Cut a long strip of gift wrap. Fold in half.

3. Fold in half again. Then open out.

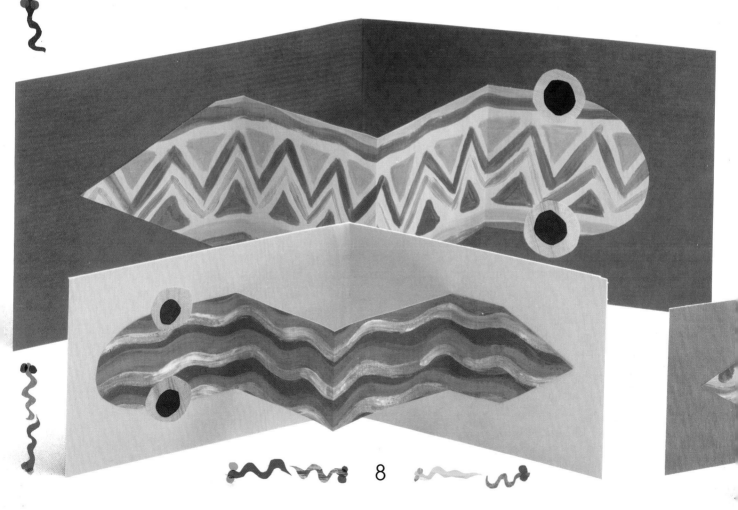

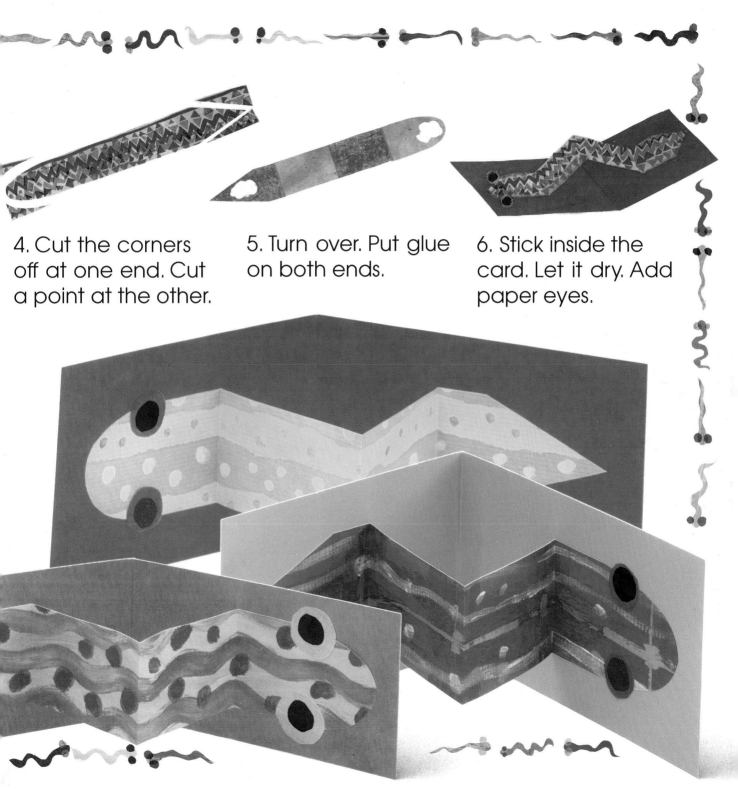

4. Cut the corners off at one end. Cut a point at the other.

5. Turn over. Put glue on both ends.

6. Stick inside the card. Let it dry. Add paper eyes.

A crown

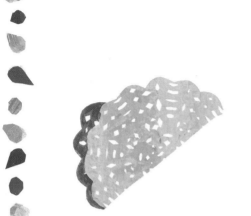

1. Fold a gold or silver doily in half.

2. Cut a strip of folded foil to fit around your head.

3. Put the folded foil inside the doily.

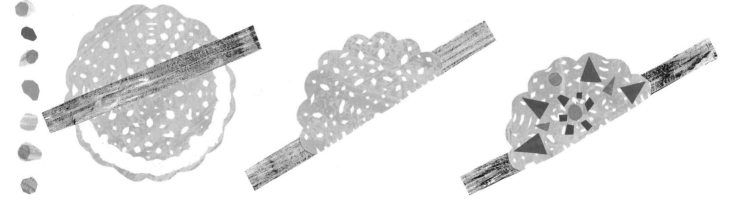

4. Open the doily. Put glue all around the bottom edge.

5. Fold it again, with the foil inside, so the sides stick.

6. Stick on scraps of shiny paper, ribbon, and crumpled tissue.

Tape the
crown to fit
your head

If you don't
have a gold or
silver doily, dab
paint on a
white one.

A hanging fish

1. Draw a fish shape on bright paper.

2. Cut it out. Glue on an eye.

3. Cut some strips. Glue them on.

Tape on a string to hang your fish up.

4. Stick on some shapes. Cut off what you don't need.

5. Cut some paper spikes. Glue them at the top.

6. Cut long pieces of tissue paper for a tail. Stick them on.

A bonfire

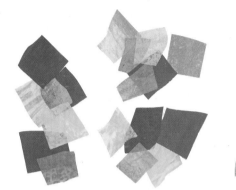

1. Cut red, orange and yellow shapes from magazines or giftwrap.

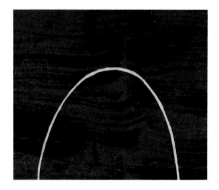

3. Draw a tall shape like a hill on dark paper.

2. Cut into flame shapes. Make the ends pointed.

4. Stick yellow flames at the top, orange flames below, then red.

5. Fill the spaces with leftover flames. Add black sticks. Cross them over.

6. Use wisps of cotton ball for smoke, and kitchen foil pieces and stars for sparks.

A spoon princess

1. Paint the back of a wooden spoon.

2. Cut cloth as wide as this book and as tall as your spoon.

3. Wrap it around the spoon. Tape at the top.

4. Fasten it on with a rubber band.

You could
stick on
sequins.

5. Tape knitting yarn to the back, then sides of the head.

6. Cut out and stick on a paper crown. Draw on a face.

An octopus puppet

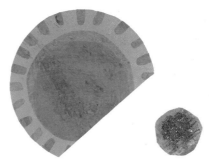

1. Cut a paper plate like this. You need both pieces.

2. Turn the big piece over. Use a sponge to wipe green paint all over.

3. Wipe green paint on both sides of a sheet of strong paper. Roll it up.

4. Cut the roll into pieces, like this. Then unroll them.

5. Stick them to the unpainted side of the plate.

6. Tape the small piece of plate to the back, for a handle.

Stick on paper
eyes and a
mouth.

You can add
some patterns
to your
octopus.

A big bug

Paint these too.

1. Cut a cardboard egg carton in two. Paint both pieces.

2. Cut the round parts from another carton, for feet.

3. Cut three pipe-cleaners in half. Stick them to the feet.

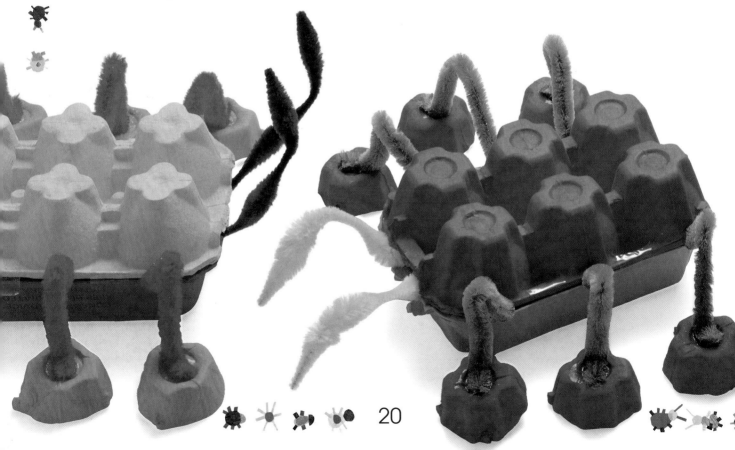

20

4. Tape these inside the flat part of the egg carton.

5. Fold a pipe-cleaner and stick it on for feelers.

6. Stick the bumpy egg carton lid on top to finish off.

A snow picture

1. Cut a cardboard circle. Paint it blue.

2. Cut tree parts from brown paper. Stick them on.

3. Cut green cloth or paper. Stick on for bushes.

4. Stick on pieces of cotton ball for snow and a snowman.

5. Add a hat, scarf and face cut from paper or cloth.

6. Stick on a kitchen foil moon, and some icicles on the tree.

Tape on a loop for hanging.

23

A pecking bird

1. Fold a paper plate. Unfold. Paint stripes on the back.

2. Fold it again. Stick a paper beak inside.

3. Cut some paper into spikes.

4. Stick them on the head. Add an eye.

Cut feather shapes and stick them on if you like.

5. Cut strips of bright tissue as long as your hand.

6. Twist them together. Tape them at the back for a tail.

Rock your bird to make it peck.

A necklace

1. Cut some paper as long as a straw. Glue the back.

2. Lay the straw in the middle. Press hard.

3. Fold the paper over the straw so the edges meet.

You could use giftwrap.

4. Press the paper hard. Let it dry. Cut it into pieces.

5. Cut shapes in the paper. Make some more.

6. Thread onto thick yarn with a big needle.

Tie the ends to fit around your neck or wrist.

A firework

1. Stick bands of paper around a toilet roll.

2. Add some sticky shapes.

3. Stick red and yellow paper onto kitchen foil. Let it dry.

4. Cut this paper into thin pieces.

5. Stick the strips inside the top.

Use a kitchen
paper towel
roll for a big
firework.

29

A big-nosed clown

1. Poke a hole in a paper plate with a pencil.

2. Wipe the back all over with bright paint. Let it dry.

3. Stick on two buttons for eyes, and a paper mouth.

4. Cut up some bright yarn and glue it on for hair.

5. Cut shapes for a hat from cardboard or a box.

6. Stick on a flower from a magazine or seed packet.

7. Get help to blow up a balloon a little way.

8. Poke it through the hole. Tape it at the back.

His nose will
wobble if you
shake his head.

A brooch

1. Draw a pig like this on stiff paper.

2. Cut it out. Stick on a button nose.

3. Tape a safety pin on the back.

You could make a fish...

...or a cat...

...or a flower.

I can crayon

Little fat birds

1. Crayon a fat body.

2. Fill in the shape. Add a beak.

3. Draw an eye near the beak. Add a wing.

This bird is feeding a worm to her baby.

4. Crayon a tail.
Give your bird some
legs.

This bird
has spiky
feathers
on its head.

Point the
wings up
for a flying
bird.

Spiders in the dark

1. Crayon a fat body.

2. Add big eyes.

3. Crayon in the body.

4. Draw 8 legs, and a thread to hang from.

5. Crayon some more spiders.

6. Cover with runny paint.

A big crane

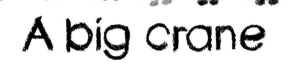

1. Crayon the cab. Leave a window hole.

2. Crayon the lifting part.

3. Draw the cable.

You could add some stripes.

4. Crayon some wheels.

5. Draw what the crane is lifting.

Draw some people.

This crane is lifting a car.

A duck card

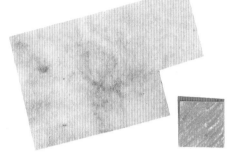

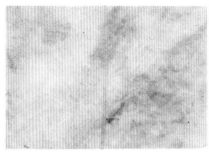

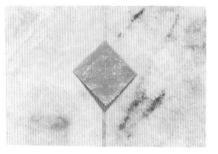

1. Cut off the corner of an envelope. Crayon the inside. Crayon the top.

2. Fold paper to make a card. Open it up again.

3. Glue the envelope corner in the middle. This makes a beak.

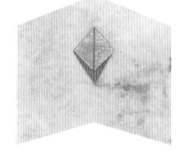

4. Lift the top up with a finger. Close the card. Squash flat.

5. Open it up. Draw a duck's head around the beak. Draw some eyes.

6. Crayon flowers and leaves around your duck.

A flower picture

1. Cut a round shape from an old birthday card.

2. Glue it onto some paper.

3. Cut out petals. Glue them on.

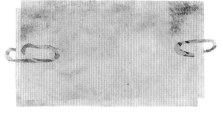

4. Clip some paper on top.

5. Rub over the flower shape with bright crayons.

You can make some leaves too.

6. Move the paper. Make more flowers.

Fireworks

1. Crayon a big firework. Press hard.

2. Add lots of sparks and squiggles.

3. Paint all over with runny dark paint.

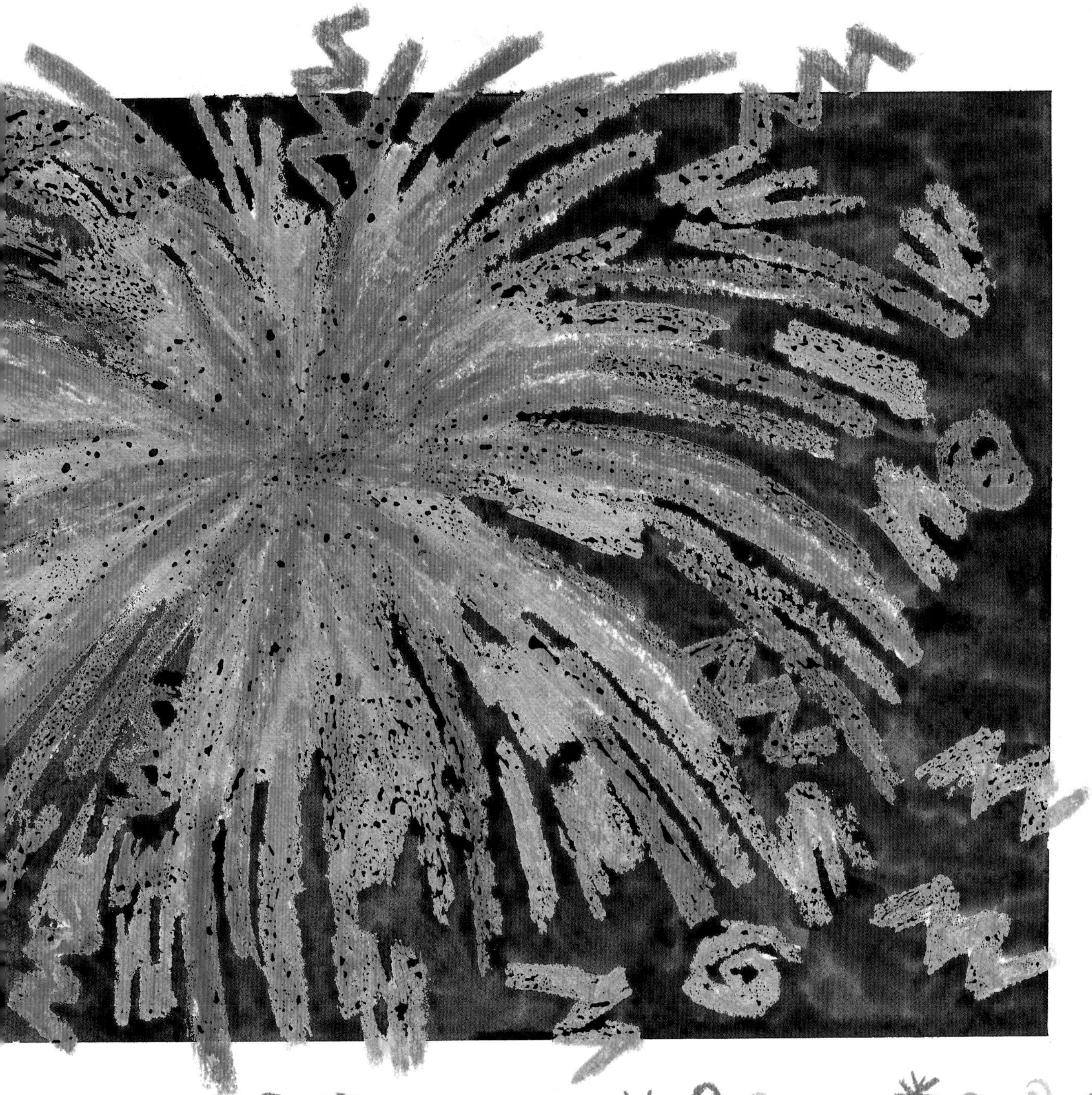

A tall giraffe

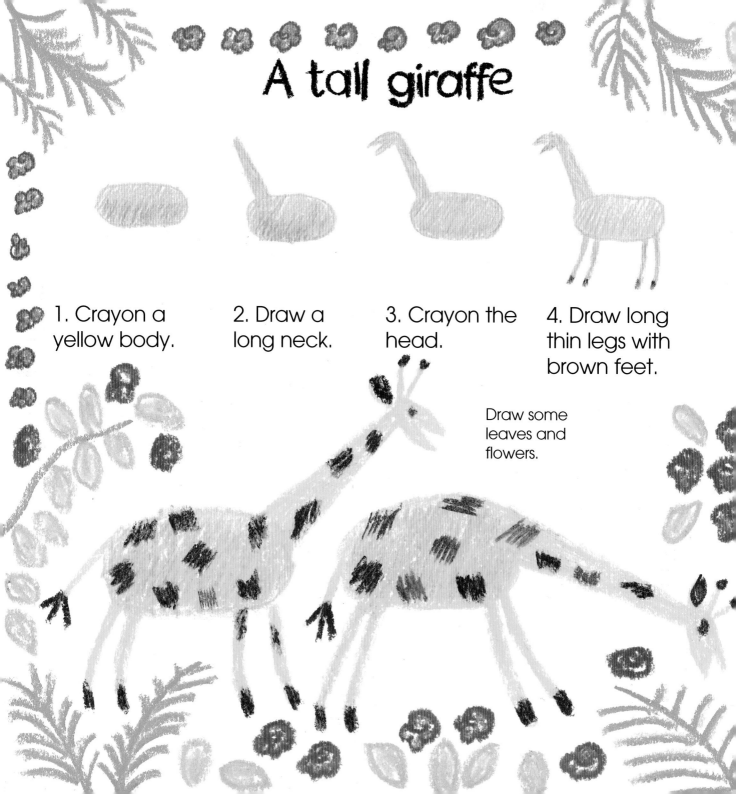

1. Crayon a yellow body.

2. Draw a long neck.

3. Crayon the head.

4. Draw long thin legs with brown feet.

Draw some leaves and flowers.

5. Add an ear and two horns.

6. Put in an eye. Add a tail, and patches.

Loopy snakes

1. Crayon patterns and stripes all over strong thin paper.

2. Cut the paper into strips - some fat, some thin.

3. Cut a thin point for a head. Cut a fat point for a tail.

You can overlap the snakes when you stick them down.

4. Put glue under the head and tail.

5. Bend and stick onto paper.

6. Stick on eyes made from circles cut in half.

A fishy scene

1. Fold thin strong paper.

2. Open it out and crayon thickly over one half.

3. Fold again. Draw a big fish with patterns, using a hard pencil.

Make
lots of
fish.

Draw some
shells too.

4. Open the paper.
Cut your fish out and
glue onto paper.

Crayon a sea
background.

Decorations

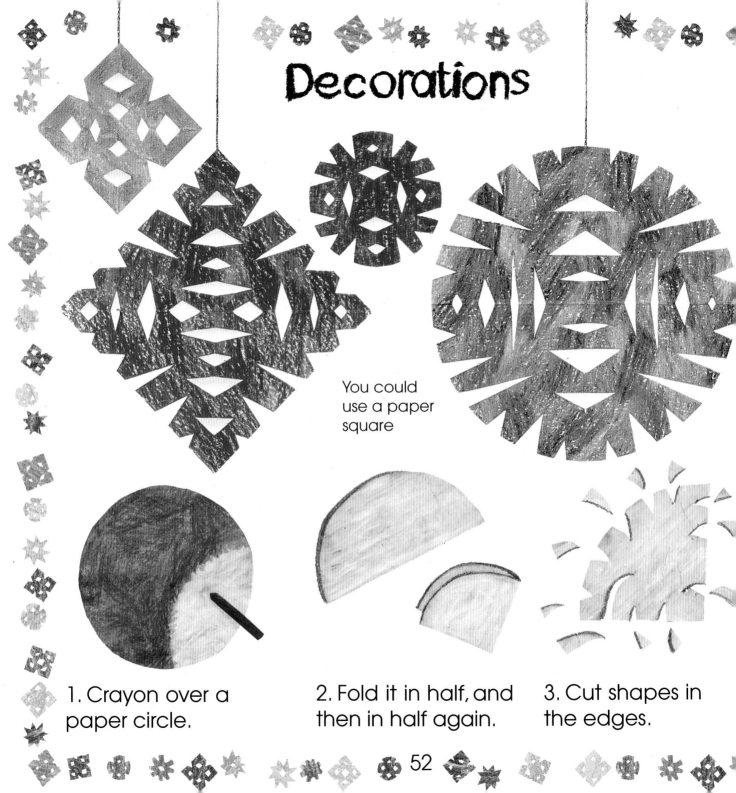

You could use a paper square

1. Crayon over a paper circle.

2. Fold it in half, and then in half again.

3. Cut shapes in the edges.

4. Open it out.

53

A caterpillar

1. Put a fat crayon on your paper, like this.

2. Push it up and down across the paper for a body.

3. Draw a head.

4. Add some eyes and a mouth.

5. Give him lots of feet, and a tail.

A piggy puppet

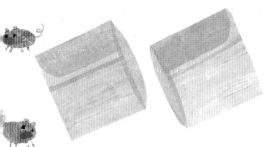 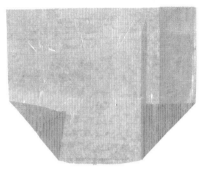 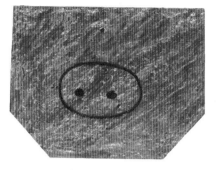

1. Stick down the flap of a long envelope. Cut it in two.

2. Fold in the corners of the open end.

3. Turn it over. Crayon the head. Add a snout.

56

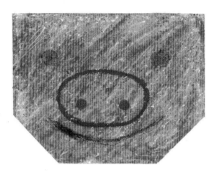

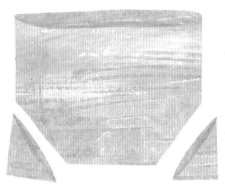

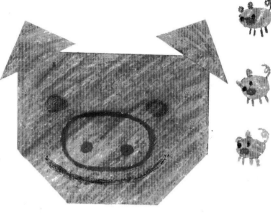

4. Draw two eyes, and a mouth.

Add big round ears for a mouse.

5. Cut the corners from the closed end of the other piece.

6. Crayon them. Glue them on.

Add big eyes for a frog.

57

Big trucks

1. Find an envelope or cut a rectangle.

2. Crayon patterns all over.

3. Paint with runny paint. Let it dry.

58

4. Glue it onto some big paper.

5. Crayon a cab at the front.

6. Add some big wheels.

Decorated eggs

1. Hard boil an egg. Crayon patterns on it.

2. Put some drops of food dye in a small bowl.

3. Put the egg in. Dab the dye all over with a paintbrush.

4. Lift it out with a spoon. Put it on paper towel to dry.

You can eat your egg if you like.

5. Put some cooking oil in a saucer.

6. Dip paper towel in the oil. Rub over the egg to make it shine.

A butterfly

1. Fold a piece of strong thin paper. Open it out.

2. Cut a card into pieces. Glue close together on one side.

3. Fold the paper again. Crayon over the top.

4. Cut the crayoned part off. Fold it. Draw two butterfly wings.

5. Cut out the wings. Open them out.

6. Crayon feelers and a body. Cut out and glue on.

Make some
leaves from
the leftovers,
or crayon
some more.

63

Lots of shapes

1. Ask a grown-up to press the sharp side of a cookie cutter into half a potato.

2. Pour some paint on an old cloth or newspaper.

3. Press the cutter in the paint and then onto some paper.

4. Make more shapes. Let them dry. Crayon them.

I can finger paint

Spotty spiders

1. Dip your finger in paint. Go around and around to make a body.

2. Draw 8 legs with a fingertip dipped in paint.

3. Do some big white eyes. Put a dark dot in the each one.

You can mix your paint with flour to make it thicker and dry quicker.

4. Dab bright spots all over.

67

Cats

1. Go around and around with a painty finger for a body.

2. Add a smaller head.

3. Do the ears and tail with a fingertip.

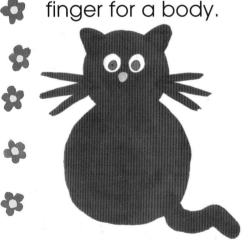

4. Add whiskers. Do eyes and nose with a fingertip.

5. Dab white paint on the cheeks, chest and feet.

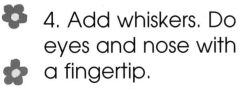

68

69

Rainbow fish

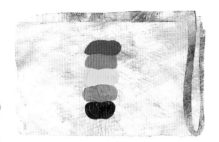

1. Spoon different paints close together on newspaper.

2. Press your hand on the paint and then on the paper.

3. Turn the shape around. Paint a tail with your finger.

4. Add an eye, and bright spots.

A folding pattern

1. Fold some paper. Open out. Press your hand in paint.

2. Press your hand on one side of the paper.

3. Wash your hands. Fold the paper. Press it all over.

4. Open out. Add more patterns on one side.

5. Fold and press again. Open it out.

6. Finger paint more patterns with different paints.

73

A rocket

1. Cut a long shape from newspaper for the rocket. Tear cloud shapes.

2. Dip them in water. Let them drip. Press them onto plain paper.

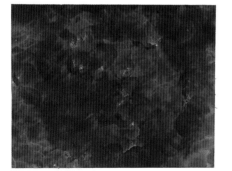

3. Pat blue paint over with your hand.

4. Peel off the newspaper shapes. Let it dry.

5. Paint the rocket's nose with a finger. Add patterns and yellow flames.

6. Do red flames on top of the yellow ones. Add stars with a fingertip.

75

Lots of flowers

1. Dip your finger in purple paint.

2. Make blue dots around the purple one.

1. Press two fingers in different paints. Go around and around.

2. Add green leaves with a finger.

1. Make a print with your thumb.

2. Make more prints underneath. Add a green stem.

An owl in a tree

1. Wet some paper with your hand. Rub yellow, orange and red paint on, like this.

2. Dip your finger in black paint. Use it to paint a tree trunk.

3. Add some long branches, using more black paint.

4. Do small branches and a hedge along the bottom.

5. Do an owl in the tree. Give him big eyes.

6. Paint a moon with your finger. Dot on some stars.

Field of rabbits

1. Press yellow handprints all over your paper. Add green handprints.

2. Finger paint a fat sausage on top for a rabbit's body.

3. Add the head.

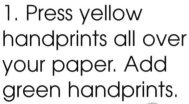

4. Finger paint ears
and legs.

5. Do a white tail.

Dab on
flowers with
a fingertip

Lots of shapes

1. Fold a piece of paper in half. Cut some shapes out of the folded side.

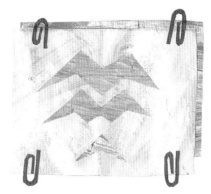

2. Open it out. Paper clip it onto another piece of paper.

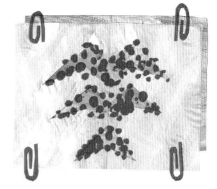

3. Dot paint over the shapes with your fingertip.

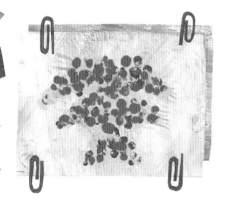

4. Dot more paint on top so the shapes are covered.

5. Lift off the top sheet to see the pattern.

83

Snails in a puddle

1. Wet some paper with your hand. Dip your fingers in paint. Make watery patterns. Let them dry.

2. Use different paper. Make a green circle with your finger.

3. Go around and around on the green with a darker green finger.

4. Add a body and horns. Let it dry. Cut out and stick onto the puddle.

An iceberg picture

1. Tear an iceberg shape from the edge of newspaper. Wet it.

2. Lay it on paper, like this. Add more shapes.

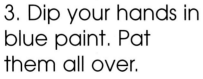

3. Dip your hands in blue paint. Pat them all over.

4. Add some green, then a little white.

5. Peel off the shapes carefully to see the icebergs.

6. Paint a canoe with a finger. Add some fishermen.

An angel

1. Make a whole handprint in the middle. This is an upside-down dress.

2. Make two whole hand prints a bit lower, for the wings.

3. Turn your paper. Go around and around with your finger for a head.

4. Use your fingertip to do arms and hands.

5. Finger paint some hair and a halo.

6. Dot on some eyes, and a nose. Paint a smiling mouth.

An alligator

1. Make a green print with the front of your fist.

2. Make more prints underneath.

3. Turn them this way. Paint the jaws with your finger.

4. Add a long tail
and four legs.

5. Make dots for
teeth along the
jaws.

6. Dot a white
eye with a black
middle.

Spiky animals

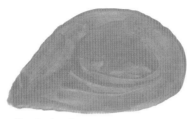

1. Dip your fingertip in paint. Go around and around for a body.

2. Make one end pointed for a snout.

3. Add an eye and a nose with your fingertip.

4. Finger paint spikes all over his back.

93

A jungle picture

1. Wet a large piece of paper. Let it drip.

2. Finger paint a green dot. Add leaves around it.

3. Do more of these in dark and light green. Leave to dry.

4. Paint a bird body with a finger. Add wings.

5. Dot a beak, the ends of the wings and tail. Add an eye.

6. Use your finger to dot on jungle flowers.

Funny creatures

1. Go around and around with a finger dipped in paint to make a blob.

2. Do spikes all around with different paint.

3. Add eyes, legs and feet with a fingertip.

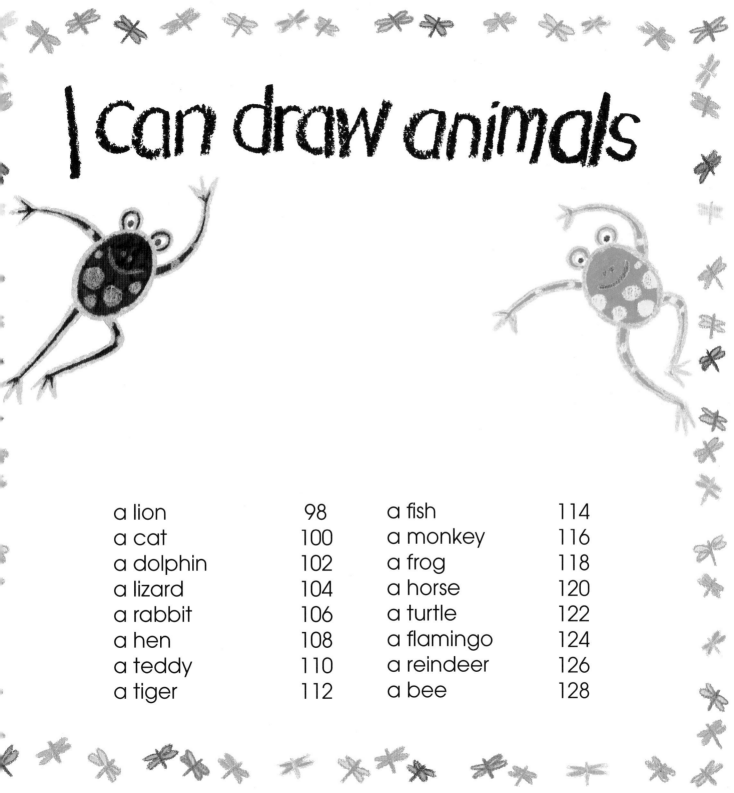

I can draw animals

a lion

1. Crayon the head.

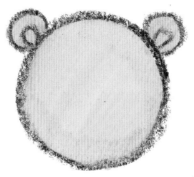

2. Add two ears. Fill in with a felt pen.

3. Crayon a nose.

4. Add the mouth and two eyes.

5. Crayon a big bushy mane all around.

6. Add whiskers.

a cat

1. Crayon a round head.

2. Crayon a fat body.

3. Add two eyes and ears.

4. Crayon the nose and mouth.

The crayon will show through.

5. Add some whiskers, and a tail.

6. Crayon stripes. Go all over with a felt pen.

a dolphin

1. Crayon a curvy line for the tummy.

2. Crayon another curve for the back.

3. Add a long nose.

4. Crayon a fin on
top and underneath.

5. Draw in an eye.
Add the mouth.

6. Crayon the tail.
Fill in with a felt pen.

103

a lizard

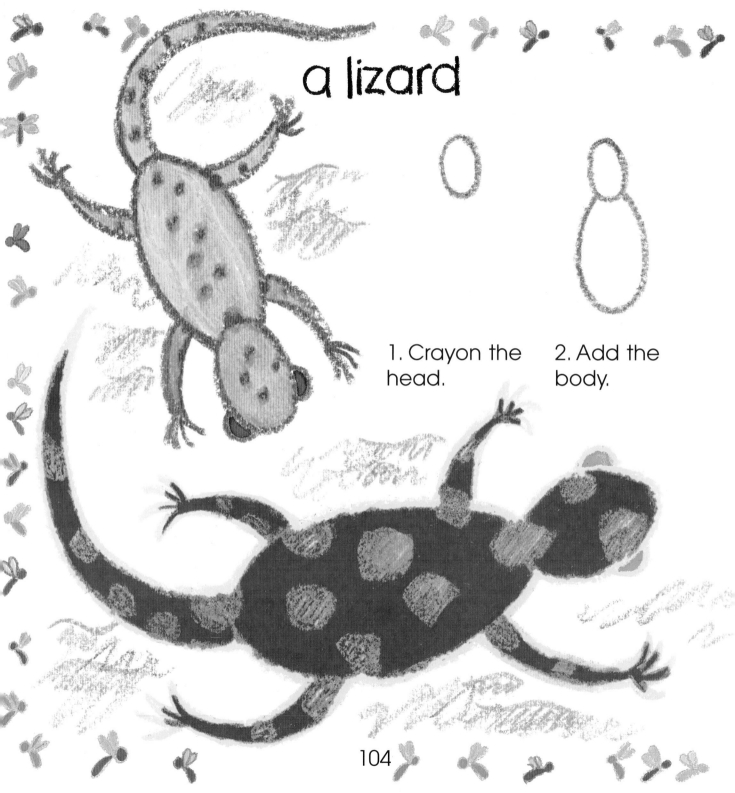

1. Crayon the head.

2. Add the body.

3. Add the
legs and eyes.

4. Add a tail
and patterns.

5. Add toes.
Go over with
a felt pen.

105

a rabbit

1. Draw a round head.

2. Add two long ears.

3. Add the body.

4. Put in eyes and a nose.

5. Draw the mouth and tail.

6. Add whiskers. Fill in with a felt pen.

106

Draw some lettuces like this.

107

a hen

1. Crayon a body.

2. Add the neck and head part.

3. Add a beak and eye. Crayon a tail.

4. Do striped legs. Crayon wing feathers.

5. Crayon the red parts. Go over your hen with a felt pen.

Draw some chicks like this.

a teddy

1. Crayon a head.

2. Add ears and a muzzle.

3. Put in the eyes, nose and mouth.

4. Crayon a fat body.

5. Add the arms.

6. Draw the legs. Fill in with a felt pen.

a tiger

1. Draw a face. Fill it in with a felt pen.

2. Put in the eyes, nose and ears.

3. Add fur around the face.

4. Crayon a long shape for a body.

5. Draw the legs and the tail. Fill in with a felt pen.

6. Crayon black stripes. Add claws and whiskers.

Draw some flowers and creepers like these.

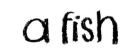

a fish

1. Crayon the body.

2. Add an eye and the mouth.

3. Crayon some patterns.

4. Go over with a felt pen.

5. Crayon a tail and two fins.

114

a monkey

1. Draw the head.

2. Add the body and a curly tail.

3. Add the muzzle and two ears.

4. Put in the eyes, nose and mouth.

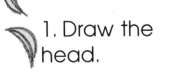

5. Do the arms and legs.

6. Add hands and feet. Fill in with a felt pen.

117

a frog

1. Crayon a body.

2. Add big eyes, a mouth and nose.

3. Crayon the front legs. Add toes.

4. Crayon the back legs. Add toes.

5. Crayon spots. Go over with a felt pen.

Draw leaping frogs like this.

a horse

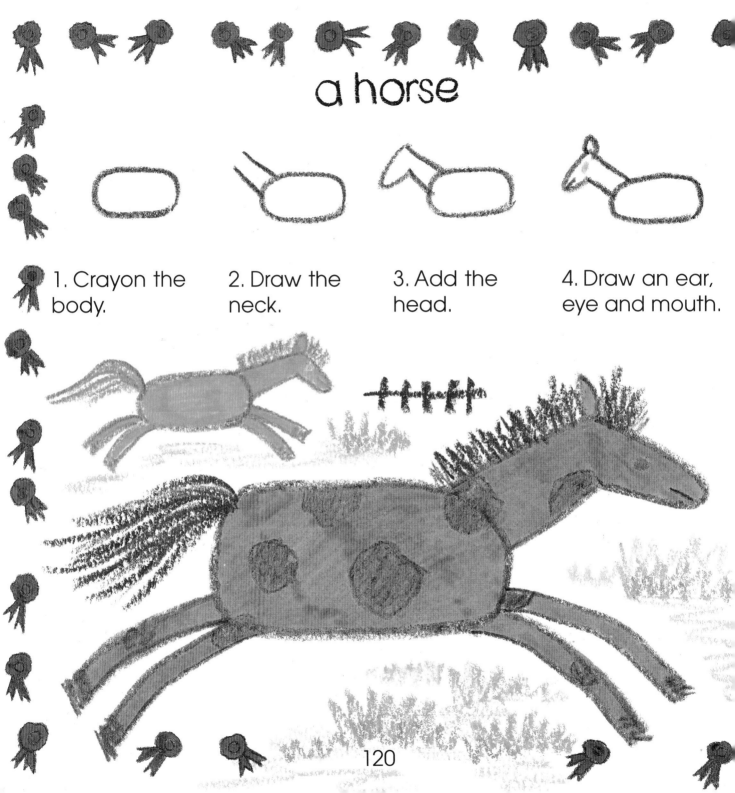

1. Crayon the body.

2. Draw the neck.

3. Add the head.

4. Draw an ear, eye and mouth.

5. Crayon four legs. Add the hooves.

6. Add a mane and tail. Fill in with a felt pen.

121

a turtle

1. Crayon a big, round shell.

2. Add the head. Put in the eyes and mouth.

3. Draw the front and back legs.

4. Add a tail. Crayon a pattern around the shell.

5. Crayon more patterns. Go over with a felt pen.

Add a sea
background

123

a flamingo

1. Crayon the body.

2. Add tail feathers and a neck.

3. Draw the head. Fill in with a felt pen.

4. Add a beak, an eye and feathers.

5. Draw long thin legs with knobbly knees.

6. Add the feet.

You could draw your flamingo standing in water.

a reindeer

1. Crayon the body. Add the neck.

2. Do the head. Add two ears.

3. Add four long legs and a tail.

4. Crayon hooves, a nose and two eyes.

5. Draw jagged antlers.

6. Add spikes to them. Fill in with a felt pen.

a bee

1. Crayon a black head.

2. Add a yellow body.

3. Crayon wings and stripes.

4. Add feelers. Fill in the wings.

First published in 1998 by Usborne Publishing Ltd, 83-85 Saffron Hill, London EC1N 8RT, England.